Solo c
shoestring

Also by Patricia Carter
An Allergy Cookbook

Solo cookery on a shoestring

by

PATRICIA CARTER

Ian Henry Publications
1983

ISBN 0 86025 871 8

Printed in England at
The Camelot Press Ltd, Southampton
for Ian Henry Publications Ltd
38 Parkstone Avenue, Hornchurch,
Essex RM11 3LW

CONTENTS

Cooking for the single person can be a nightmare or it may be simple, easy and pleasant.

Quick, easy meals for the person on his or her own can mean cups of tea or coffee and fish and chips. To some, it isn't even that.

It is no wonder that, in time, that individual becomes run down and subject to any illness that is going around at the time.

Some people living in 'bed-sits' have nothing more than a gas ring, with just a frying pan or saucepan to cook in and they can hardly imagine how anyone can make quick, nourishing, easy meals with such basic equipment - and not too much fuss.

This book is designed for such people, as well as those who have more sophisticated equipment. Most of the recipes take no more than 15-20 minutes to prepare and cook, but I have included some casseroles that take about one hour, including preparation.

Most greengrocers will sell small quantities of fruit and vegetables: I often go in and ask for one apple or orange. Health Food Stores will also sell small portions of dried peas, beans and other pulses. Look out for small tins, about 6-7 oz. in weight, of fruit, vegetables, meat and fish in large super-markets. Don't be afraid to go up to the section that sells cold meats, etc., to ask for 2 or 3 rashers of bacon - or even the off-cuts that are much cheaper.

You don't need fancy storage jars to keep things in. I use jam jars, yoghurt and margarine cartons, and label them.

If you are just starting up, you need a frying pan with lid and a saucepan with lid. Apart from these, a Swiss roll tin, a wooden spoon, an egg whisk, a baking pan, a rolling pin, a tin opener, and a 1 lb loaf tin, plus some bun tins, are all that is necessary. You can always build up from there if you need to.

If you possess a Chinese 'Wok', good; and a blender or liquidiser, even better. Apart from the attractive appearance of fireproof dishes, these are very practical, as you can use them straight from the oven.

Naturally, a refrigerator and a freezer are an asset, alternatively, a refrigerator with a freezing compartment at the top. Most of them keep food for up to three months, which is quite adequate to get through the worst of a winter.

If you can, make up twice the quantity stated in a recipe, then put half into cartons or plastic bags, label, and keep for another day when you are too busy or, maybe, not feeling well enough to cook. All the recipes in this book will freeze successfully

Quickly cooked food retains all the nourishment, as well as precious vitamins and minerals that are vital for well-being and good health.I have tried to get away from the old habit of boiling vegetables for lengthy times, covered in too much water. Most of these recipes are cooked quickly in a shallow pan with a lid and very little water.

Having said all this, there is nothing wrong in buying frozen and pre-packed foods, providing fresh fruit and vegetables are eaten every day. After all, salads need no cooking and they are time saving. Dairy produce is most beneficial and, contrary to all the fads about putting on weight, milk and eggs are not fattening. Cheese may be, however. It is usually what accompanies them that adds weight. Sugar is also fattening, although a certain amount is needed for warmth and energy.

The general rule is - nothing in excess. Well balanced, nourishing, as well as attractive, dishes all make for good health.

Both mint and parsley can be grown in pots on a window sill. Alfalfa, bean shoots and other sprouting seeds can be grown in a seeder or jar. Simply put about 1 tablespoonful of alfalfa seeds in a jar, cover with muslin and tie tightly. Run tepid water into the jar and shake gently, then drain off the water. Then run under cold water two or three times, twice a day. At the end of 7 days you will have lovely sprouts of alfalfa. Put this into sandwiches, just like mustard and cress, with salt and pepper. It is highly nutritious. Of course, you can grow mustard and cress in the same way.

Just a note to the newly widowed. It is wise to have a good clear-out of all store cupboards and throw away all unmarked and opened tatty packages, and start afresh. This will enable you to know where everything is - and you will find that you didn't need half the things anyway. After this, take stock of the most essential items and start again.

OVEN TEMPERATURES
(in electric and gas)

F	C	Gas mark	Temperature
250	130	½	Very cool
275	140	1	Very cool
300	150	2	Cool
325	165	3	Warm
350	180	4	Moderate
375	190	5	Fairly hot
400	200	6	Fairly hot
425	215	7	Hot
450	230	8	Very hot
475	240	9	Very hot

All the recipes in this book show the metric as well as the Imperial measures, e.g. 50 g. or 2 oz. It is very important to use either the metric or the Imperial measures, as the proportions will be slightly different. For example, if the recipe says 50 g. - 2 oz plain flour, either use the g. on the left hand side or the oz. on the right hand. Do not mix the methods.

WEIGHTS

The metric unit is the kilogram which equals 1,000 grams (g), or approximately 2 lb 4 oz.

Metric	Approx Imperial equivalent
25 g	1 oz
50 g	2 oz
75 g	3 oz
100 - 125 g	4 oz
150 g	5 oz
200 oz	7 oz
225 g	8 oz
250 g	9 oz
275 g	10 oz
300 g	11 oz
325 - 350 g	12 oz
375 g	13 oz
400 g	14 oz
425 g	15 oz
450 g	16 oz (1 lb)
500 g (½ kg)	17½ oz
1 kg	2.2 lb
1.5 kg	3.3 lb
2 kg	4.4 lb
2.5 kg	5½ lb

3 kg	6.6 lb
3.5 kg	7.7 lb
4 kg	8.8 lb
4.5 kg	9.9 lb
5 kg	11 lb

Standard Measuring Spoons

The level metric capacity of a spoon (British Imperial Standard) is approximately as follows -

20 ml	4 teaspoons (opt.)
15 ml	1 tablespoon
10 ml	2 teaspoons
5 ml	1 teaspoon
2.5 ml	½ teaspoon
1.25 ml	¼ teaspoon

Liquid Capacity

The standard metric unit is -
The litre (l.), which contains 100 decilitres (dl.) or 1000 millilitres (ml.). The litre is equivalent to 1¾ pints or 35 fluid oz.

Metric	Approx. Imperial equivalent
25 ml.	1 fluid oz.
50 ml.	2 fluid oz.
100 ml. (1 dl.)	4 fluid oz.
150 ml.	5 fluid oz.
300 ml.	10 fluid oz.
600 ml.	20 fluid oz (1 pint)
1000 ml. (1 l.)	35 fluid oz.

BASICS FOR YOUR STORE CUPBOARD

Dried Food

Self raising and Plain flour
Sugar
Tea
Coffee
Dried milk
Coffee-mate
Cocoa
Salt
Pepper
Baking powder
Bicarbonate of soda
Cornflour
Rice
Macaroni
Dried peas, beans and lentils
Breadcrumbs or Wheatgerm
Dried onions
Mixed dried vegetables
Batter or Yorkshire pudding mix
Dried fruit
Packets of soup mix

Tinned Foods

FRUIT
Pineapple
Peaches
Apricots
Prunes
Pie fillings

VEGETABLES

Italian tomatoes
Mushrooms
Sweet corn
New potatoes
Peas

FISH

Sardines
Soft roes
Anchovies
Salmon
Tuna

MEAT

Spam
Chopped ham
Pate
Luncheon meat
Small puddings

MILK

Condensed
Evaporated

HERBS, SPICES AND SEASONINGS

Bay leaves
Bouquet garni (small packets of 6 sachets)
Dried mint and parsley

Oregano
Ginger
Mixed spices
Cayenne pepper
Stock cubes
Dry mustard
Vanilla and Almond essence
Sage and onion stuffing
Parsley and thyme stuffing
Curry powder

PRESERVES AND BOTTLED SAUCES

Jams
Syrup
Honey
Bovril
Marmite
Tomato juice
Tomato ketchup
Worcestershire sauce
Tomato puree

Although these are the most important items you will need for a good storecupboard, you might like to add a few more of your own choice. It may look a long list of ingredients if you have a limited amount of space, but most of the things are quite small. Flour can be bought in 1.1 lb (450 g) bags, but, apart from sugar sold in bags of 2.2 oz., the rest of the items take up very little space. With good stacking and organisation, you won't need a lot of cupboards, especially if you have a small refrigerator.

HINTS AND TIPS

1. Ask your milkman if he carries other items besides milk, such as bread, cream, yoghurt, potatoes and eggs. Many of the larger dairy combines do have this facility.
2. $\frac{1}{2}$ lb. of butter or margerine (225 g) can be cut into half, 4 oz (100–125 g), then in half again, 2 oz (50 g). This is handy for measuring fat for cakes or pastry.
3. Save plastic cartons and jars for storing dried fruit, peas and beans, etc.
4. A few grains of uncooked rice placed in a salt shaker wil absorb dampness.
5. To make icing sugar when you have run out. Place some granulated sugar in a liquidiser, or in a plastic bag and roll with a rolling pin.
6. Stale rolls or bread sprinkled with water and placed in the oven for about 10 minutes will come out as good as new.
7. When cooking greens, a few drops of vinegar will get rid of the smell.
8. Keep some candles in case of power cuts and other emergencies.
9. Don't throw outer leaves of lettuce away, they make excellent soup. See recipe.
10. Check store from time to time for old opened packets and replace with new ones.

11. Use leftover pastry for jam or cheese turnovers.

12. Check refrigerator or cooler for such items as flour, sugar, butter, margerine, onions and garlic after trying a recipe and replace where necessary.

13. Check refrigerator each week for such items as butter, margerine, eggs, fruit and vegetables, meat and fish, and re-order.

14. Any leftover cream or yoghurt can be used for next meal.

15. Once tinned food has been opened, use within 24 hours and store in a cool place.

16. To keep bread fresh, store in a plastic bag in refrigerator or cooler.

17. To make breadcrumbs, toast stale bread slowly until lightly brown, cool, then break toast up into small pieces, put them in a paper bag and roll with a rolling pin till bread is fine crumbs. Alternatively, put toast into blender for a few seconds. Store in a plastic bag in freezer or keep in jar in refrigerator.

18. Do make sure that frozen meat is thoroughly thawed out before cooking, especially chicken. Otherwise the outside can get cooked first, leaving the inside raw. This can lead to a risk of food poisoning.

19. One British pint is 20 fluid ounces, but the American pint is 16 fluid ounces. Also 1 cup (in dry measure) is 8 ounces, not 10 ounces.

20. If you are in a hurry with no time to make pastry, you can buy frozen puff pastry and short crust pastry. They can also be bought in packets.

21. Criossants are an excellent substitute for

pastry. Just place in a warm oven for a few moments and serve with cooked fruit and savoury dishes.

22. A sugar lump placed in a biscuit tin will keep the biscuits from going soft.

23. A pinch of salt on a sour apple will take away the tartness.

24. A cube of flavoured jelly will improve rhubarb or similar sharp fruit.

METHODS OF COOKING MEAT

Choice of meat

Beef: Good beef should be bright red in colour. Fat should be creamy with streaks distributed evenly throughout the lean.

Lamb: The flesh should be pinkish in colour and fat white and firm.

Mutton: Flesh should be dark red and firm. Fat should be white.

Pork: The fat should be white and the flesh pinkish.

Veal: Light greyish-pink in colour.

Frozen meat

All frozen meat should be properly defrosted at normal room temperature slowly.

Boiling

Dice meat, put into boiling water together with chopped vegetables. Boil for 5 - 10 minutes, reduce heat and simmer slowly until quite tender.

Braising

Toss the meat in flour and fry in a pan for a few minutes on each side, using vegetable oil. Add a bouquet garni, salt and pepper to taste, add ½ pint water, cover with lid and simmer for 20 - 25 minutes, or till tender, just above the centre of oven 190 - 375F - Gas Mark 5. Chopped vegetables of choice should be added for a complete meal.

Dry frying

This is very good for such meat as sausages, chops, steaks, etc. Oil frying pan over a high heat for a few minutes, reduce heat, then finish cooking over slow heat. It is advisable to prick sausages before cooking to prevent bursting.

Grilling

The grill should be red hot before placing food under it.

1. Brush meat with vegetable oil, add salt and pepper, oil bars of grid to prevent meat sticking.

2. Beat steak before grilling, as this breaks down fibre, thus making it more tender. Grill meat on full heat for 2 mins, reduce heat.
3. Then cook for stated times on chart below -

MEAT	PREPARATION	COOKING TIME
Rump steak 1-1½" thick	Beat, cover both sides in oil	7 - 10 mins each side
Fillet steak 1-2" thick	Beat, cover both sides in oil	7 - 10 mins each side
Loin chops 1" thick	Bone & skin, roll & skewer	5 - 6 min each side
Pork chops	Slightly longer cooking	
Sausage	Prick each side	10-15 min
Bacon	Remove rind & fat	3-6 mins
Liver	Wash, roll in flour in oiled pan	15-20 min
Kidneys	Wash, wipe, remove ducts & fat. Slice.	5-8 mins

TEST FOR GRILLING

1. Surface of meat should be slightly puffy in appearance.
2. Steak should show a little blood when pressed.
3. Pork should be well done.
4. Lamb should also be fairly well done.

ROASTING

Times

Beef: 20 min per lb (450 g) and 20 min. extra.
Lamb: 25 min per lb. (450 g) and 25 min extra.
Mutton: as for lamb.
Pork: 30 min per lb (450 g) and 30 min extra.
Veal: as for pork.
Stuffed meat: 35 min per lb (450 g) and 35 min extra.

PREPARATION OF ROASTING

Heat oven to required time, oil pan well, cover meat with foil and cook for stated time. Skewer and tie with clean string if necessary.

STEWING

This is a good method for cooking the tougher cuts of meat. Meat must be chopped into small pieces and boiled for at least 1 hour - and even 2, if the meat if really tough. The lid must be kept on tightly, throughout cooking.

METHODS OF COOKING FISH

[Assuming ½lb of fish]

Boiling

Put fish in pan of hot water and stand fish on an upturned small foil pie dish. Season with salt and pepper and add a little lemon juice or vinegar. Cover with lid, bring to boil, reduce heat and simmer for 10 to 15 minutes, or until soft. Test with fork or skewer.

Deep frying

Use pan with wire basket and heat vegetable oil until it is smokey hot. Coat fish with flour, dip in beaten egg, then roll fish in either wheatgerm or breadcrumbs. Fry until golden brown.

Grilling

Oil the wire stand in the grill pan and heat the grill. Pol fish in margarine or oil and grill, with the flesh side up first. Turn fish over and grill other side. About 7 to 10 minutes.

Shallow frying

Heat small amount of vegetable oil in frying pan till smokey hot. Roll fish in flour, then dip in beaten egg. Then roll in either wheatgerm or breadcrumbs. Fry fish till golden brown on both sides.

Steaming

Bring water to boil in a fairly deep pan. About ½ pint [275-300 ml.] Wrap fish in foil, season with salt and pepper, and immerse fish into water. Steam for 15 to 20 minutes, or until soft. Test with a fork or skewer. A little vinegar or lemon juice may be added before cooking.

METHODS OF PREPARING & COOKING VEGETABLES

Vegetables should be cooked as little as possible and in very little water. This way all the vitamins and minerals are not lost and discarded with excess water down the drain.

Carrots and potatoes should be scraped instead of peeling. Take only the very brown or dirtiest leaves off sprouts, spinach, cabbage, lettuce, etc. These outer leaves usually contain most of the goodness and it is a shame to throw these away if they look reasonably clean and crisp.

Do not use soda as this destroys the vitamin content. It is better if salt is added near the end of cooking if possible.

If you possess a 'wok' and use it as directed, all vegetables will be much more tasty, as they are cooked for as short a time as possible.

in the recipes for vegetables throughout this book, all have been lightly done in a pan with a lid which is similar to cooking in a wok.

Do try and vary your diet and have different vegetables every day.

Nearly all vegetables, if diced up small or sliced very thinly, will need no more cooking than 5 to 10 minutes in a pan with a small quantity of water and a tightly fitting lid.

LUNCH OR DINNER MENUS FOR 2 WEEKS

<u>Day 1</u>
Soup
Frying pan souffle, with vegetables
Raspberry cream ripple

<u>Day 2</u>
Fruit or Tomato juice
Grilled gammon, peach with spiced cream and peas
Cheese and biscuits

<u>Day 3</u>
Soup
Brunch
Fresh fruit

<u>Day 4</u>
Tomato juice
Grilled chop and small salad
Fruit and cream or Yoghurt

<u>Day 5</u>
Fruit juice
Fish and chips or Fish and creamed potatoes, and peas or beans
Fresh fruit or Ice cream

<u>Day 6</u>
Soup
Liver and bacon with noodles or rice and vegetables
Fresh fruit

<u>Day 7</u>
Grapefruit segments on lettuce
Steak and chips or mashed potato with a small salad

<u>Day 8</u>
Fruit juice
Roast lamb with roast potato and vegetables
Semolina or Rice pudding

Day 9
Soup
Cold leftover meat and small salad
Marshmellow chocolate dessert

Day 10
Melon
Omelet with chopped mixed vegetables
Cheese and biscuits or Ice cream

Day 11
Starter
Grilled sausages and bacon with small salad
Ice cream

Day 12
Soup
Poached haddock with sauce and peas
Tricia's chocolate cream surprise

Day 13
Fruit juice
Chicken and ham with white wine sauce and potato baked in jacket
Cheese and biscuits

Day 14
Soup
Kebabs with a small salad
Fruit yoghurt or Ice cream

All the above can be found in this book either in the recipe sections following or in the methods of preparing meat, fish or vegetables. The only exceptions to this are things like fish and chips: it is quicker to buy these than to cook them yourself.

Salads

These are the dishes that never boost the fuel bill and the ones that are best all round for us all.
Nicely and thoughtfully prepared in an atrractive manner, salads can be the best meal of all - especially if mixed with fresh fruit as well as meat, fish or cheese. Garnished with fresh herbs and dressings they are deicious. Be adventurous and creative.

Here are some popular ingredients for good nourishing salads; perhaps you can think of some more of your own choice.
Mix and Match Salads (choose any from the list)

Watercress
Beetroot (diced)
Cabbage (raw, sliced, washed thoroughly and mixed with quick salad dressing or mayonnaise)
Carrot (raw, scraped and shredded)

Cauliflower (broken into small pieces & washed)
Celery sticks, stuffed with cream cheese
Chinese lettuce (shredded and washed)
Cucumber (sliced)
Cottage cheese
Egg (hardboiled, sliced. Boil for 10 mins. Cool in cold water and peel)
Lettuce (various types, washed and sliced or shredded)
Radishes (top & tail removed, washed & sliced)
Spring onions (snip off ends, and wash)
Potatoes (boiled for 10 mins, drained & mashed with milk)
Tomatoes (washed and sliced)
Mustard & cress
Canteloupe melon (deseeded & sliced or cut into 1" chunks)
Peach halves or slices
Pineapple rings
Eating apple (sliced with skin)
Fish
Cheeses (various)
Cold meats (various)
Chopped nuts (various)
Quick salad dressing (see recipe)
Quick vinaigrette (see recipe)
Pears (washed, cored and sliced or halved with cream and nuts)

This is my own list, but be adventurous and add some of your own.

Examples of how to make up an attractive salad

NUMBER ONE

Arrange some Chinese lettuce round a plate. 1 pineapple ring and 1 peach half, topped with cottage cheese or whipped cream with chopped nuts and garnished with sweet basil or celery salt. 1 carrot, scraped and shredded. Cucumber slices round carrot. 1 boiled potato.
Put potato in an icing bag with a wide icing nozzle and pipe rosettes round the outer edge of salad. Sprinkle a little cayenne over top of each rosette and serve with vinaigrette or Quick salad dressing.

NUMBER TWO

Small quantities of raw cabbage, shredded carrot cucumber and tomato. 1 peach half, a pear half. 1 tin of sardines (or other fish). Olives.
Wash all ingredients. Arrange cabbage, carrots and cucumber round the plate. Cover sardines with dressing of choice and garnish with flaked almonds and olives (if you have any!). Fill centres of peach and pear with cream or yoghurt and garnish with mixed spice.

QUICK SALAD DRESSING

2 or 3 tblsp	Single cream or Plain yoghurt
½ teasp	Dry or French mustard
	Salt and pepper to taste
Pinch of	Rosemary, thyme, celery salt, tarragon and finely chopped mint or parsley

Blend all together and spoon over salad.

VINAIGRETTE

2 tblsp	Sunflower oil or Olive oil
2 teasp	White vinegar or Lemon juice
	Salt & pepper
Pinch of	Dill, chili powder, tarragon, celery salt.

Mix all the ingredients together and keep in a small jar, in the refrigerator.

Soups & Starters

Apart from a couple, the soups here are very quick and easy to prepare. If you have a refrigerator or a freezer, it is time saving (as well as saving on the fuel bill) to make twice the quantity and either freeze or keep some in the 'fridge for next day.
All the soups will freeze well and, of course, if you are in a hurry or just don't want the bother of cooking - unfreeze a carton of soup, reboil and serve.
The starters I have given are all well balanced nutritionally and make very good lunch snacks as well, especially with a bowl of soup to start with and with a nice crusty roll.

CARROT SOUP

6	Large carrots (scraped & minced)
1 pint	Water [575-600 ml]
1	Small onion (chopped)
3 slices	Bacon (rinds removed)
1	Bay leaf
	Salt & pepper
½ teasp	Brown sugar
Pinch of	Nutmeg

Method

Place all ingredients in a saucepan. Bring to boil. Reduce heat, cover with lid and simmer gently for 20 mins. Remove bay leaf. Cool and blend or put through a sieve. Return soup to saucepan. Bring to boil, reduce heat and simmer for 5 mins.
Serve with croutons.

****

To make croutons, fry a slice of bread in margarine or vegetable oil, then cut into square chunks.
25 minutes.

LENTIL SOUP

3 slices	Bacon (rinds removed)	
4 tblsp	Lentils (soaked ½ hour earlier)	
1	Small onion (chopped)	
	Salt and pepper	
1	Bay leaf	
1 pint	Water	[575-600 ml]

Method

Fry and mince bacon, place all ingredients in saucepan. Bring to boil, reduce heat and simmer gently with lid on for 1 hour. Cool. Remove bay leaf. Put in blender or mince lentils and return to saucepan. Bring to boil. Reduce heat and simmer for 10 minutes.
1 hour, 10 minutes.

ONION SOUP

2	Large onions (minced or chopped)	
2 slices	Bacon (rind removed)	
1	Sachet of bouquet garni	
	Salt & pepper	
1 pint	Water	[575-600 ml]
1 tblsp	Cream	
	Watercress (for garnish)	

Method

Please all ingredients, except cream and water-cress, in saucepan. Bring to boil, reduce heat, cover with lid, and simmer for ½ hour. Cool and blend or put through sieve. Return soup to saucepan. Bring to boil, reduce heat and simmer for 5 mins. Add cream and serve with a sprig of watercress.
10 minutes.

LETTUCE SOUP

All the outer leaves of a lettuce. It really doesn't matter how many leaves. Break them up into fairly small pieces, wash thoroughly, place in quite a large saucepan. Add about 1 pint [575 - 600 ml] of water. Peel and chop one small onion and, if liked, a clove of garlic, crushed. Salt and pepper to taste and a good pinch of oregano (optional). Press down lettuce, cover with a lid, bring to boil, reduce heat and simmer for 20 mins. Let soup cool, either sieve or put in a liquidiser for a couple of minutes. Serve with croutons. (For croutons see page 26).
20 minutes

MIXED VEGETABLE SOUP

Method

Soak 1 tblsp each of butter beans, dried peas and lentils for about 8 hours. Drain them. Place these, a ham bone and a chopped onion, carrot, tomato, a couple of sticks of celery, one potato, one tblsp pearl barley, a small swede (optional) and a stock cube. Salt & pepper to taste.
Cover with water, add a bouquet garni. Bring to boil. Reduce heat, cover with lid, and simmer for 1 hour. Remove bouquet garni and ham bone. Cool, put through sieve or blender. Return soup to saucepan, bring to boil and then simmer for further 5 mins. Add a little cream and serve with croutons. (For croutons see page 26)
Time (excluding soaking of pulses) 1 hour, 10 minutes

AVOCADO WITH EGG

1	Avocado pear (sliced in half and stone removed)
1	Egg (hard boiled)
1 tblsp	Double cream
	Salt and pepper to taste
A good pinch	Paprika for garnishing
1 tblsp	Brandy or Sherry (optional)
1	Tomato (sliced)
Few leaves	Lettuce
Few slices	Cucumber for garnishing

Method

Scoop out flesh from avocado halves and save the skin. Mix brandy (or sherry) with cream. Mash egg and add salt and pepper to taste. Now blend all the ingredients together and spoon back into avocado skins. Put the halves on a bed of shredded lettuce and garnish with tomato and cucumber; lastly sprinkle paprika over top.
5 - 7 minutes.

CHICKEN LIVER PATE

½ teasp	Sugar
1 slice	Bacon (fat removed, chopped)
8 oz	Chicken livers (sliced thinly and any membrane removed) [225 g]
1 level tblsp	Margarine
1	Small onion
1	Bay leaf
	Salt & pepper
1 teasp	Worcestershire sauce
1 clove	Garlic
1 level teasp	Dry mustard
1 tblsp	Brandy

Method

Peel and chop onion and lightly fry in margarine. Add rest of ingredients and simmer for about 5 mins with lid on until liver is cooked. Remove bay leaf. Either mince twice or liquidise until smooth. Cool. Place pate in clean carton, cover with lide and keep in fridge or freezer. Serve on bed of lettuce with thin slices of toast.
10 - 15 minutes.

QUICK PATE

2 oz	Liver sausage	[50 g]
1	Egg (hard boiled)	
1 tblsp	Sandwich spread	
1 tblsp	Double cream	
A little	White wine	

Method

Mix all the ingredients together and form into a cone. Serve on bed of lettuce. Garnish with parsley or watercress.

SARDINE MAYONNAISE

1 tin	Sardines (remove excess oil)
1 tblsp	Mayonnaise
A few	Stuffed olives
	Salt & pepper to taste
Sprinkling	Dill seeds and fennel seeds (optional)
1	Tomato (sliced)
Few leaves	Lettuce

Method

Lay sardines on lettuce, then spoon mayonnaise over top. Sprinkle dill and fennel seeds over mayonnaise and lay olives over the top. Garnish with tomato.
5 - 7 minutes.

STUFFED ROLLED HAM

2 slices	Ham
1 tblsp	Mayonnaise or Double cream
2 tblsp	Mixed diced vegetables (tomato, cucumber, radish, beetroot, etc.)
	Salt & pepper to taste
Pinch of	Cayenne pepper and curry powder
A few	Lettuce leaves (shredded)
Few	Olives for garnishing (optional)
1 or 2	Slices of peach

Method

Mix mayonnaise (or cream) with diced vegetables, salt and pepper, curry powder and Cayenne pepper. Spoon mixture into each of the slices of ham and roll. Lay them on the lettuce and garnish with olives (if you are using them)
5 - 7 minutes

Savoury dishes

The aim of these dishes is to provide a good, and substantial, as well as nourishing meal, in as short a time as possible. Obviously, the casseroles take longer to cook, but most of the recipes require only 20 - 25 minutes to prepare, including the cooking.

BOILED RICE

1 heaped tblsp Long grain rice
A couple of drops of yellow colouring or
A little saffron to colour (optional)
Salt & pepper

Method

Cover rice with water and add salt and pepper. Bring to boil. Reduce heat and simmer until soft or until water has nearly gone - about 10 mins. Drain off water and serve. Pasta - that is, macaroni, noodles or spaghetii - can be cooked in a smiliar fashion.
12 - 15 minutes.

BRUNCH

Brunch is a mixture of a lot of cooked meats and vegetables. Here is mine -

2	Sausages
1 slice	Bacon
1	Kidney (sinew removed) (optional)
Few slices	Black pudding (also optional)
Couple	Mushrooms
1	Tomato
1 or 2	Eggs
	French fried potatoes (Chips)

Method

Oil a frying pan and start the sausages first, then gradually add the other ingredients. As they cook, remove them and keep them warm under the grill till the last ingredients are cooked. It is wise to leave the eggs till last, as these will go hard under the grill. At the same time, fry potatoes in oil until golden brown.

CELEBRATION SALMON

1 cutlet	Pink or Red fresh Scotch salmon
A little	Vegetable oil
	Salt & pepper
½ carton	Double cream (small) [60 ml, 2½ oz]
	Finely grated rind of medium lemon

Method

Oil a fairly small fire proof casserole with vegetable oil. Place salmon in dish. Add salt and pepper. Fold finely grated lemon peel into cream with a fork. Pour cream over salmon. Cover with lid or foil and bake for 25 mins just above centre of oven. 180, 350F, Gas Mark 4. Serve with peas or green beans and boiled minted potatoes.
30 minutes.

Any cream left over may be used for quick dessert (see pages 74-80).

CHICKEN AND HAM IN WHITE WINE SAUCE

1 heaped tblsp	Breadcrumbs or wheatgerm	
2	Chicken drumsticks (skinned)	
1	Stock cube	
6 tblsp	Water	
2 tblsp	White wine	
1	Small onion (chopped)	
2 oz	Mushrooms (chopped)	[50 g]
2 oz	Chopped ham	[50 g]
1	Bay leaf	
	Salt & pepper to taste	
1 level tblsp	Plain flour	
2 tblsp	Cream	

Method

Mix stock cube with water, dip drumsticks in stock, then roll in crumbs or wheatgerm. Put these and rest of ingredients, except flour and cream, into casserole. Cover with lid or foil. Put in oven just above centre and bake for 1 hour at 180, 370F, Gas Mark 4. Towards end of cooking, mix flour with a little water and stir into casserole. Cook for a further ten minutes. Remove bay leaf, add cream and serve.

While you are using the oven, it is a good idea to cook another dish at the same time. Wash and scrub one medium-sized potato. Wrap it in foil and bake for the same length of time. Or peel a medium-sized potato, cut into quarters, heat 2 or 3 tablespoons of oil in a small fire-proof dish or pan. Put potatoes in pan and bake them for ½ hour.
1 hour, 15 minutes.

CHICKEN WITH PARSLEY SAUCE

2 heaped tblsp	Wheatgerm or breadcrumbs seasoned with salt & pepper
2	Chicken drumsticks (skinned)
1 tblsp	Vegetable oil
1	Egg (beaten)

Method

Heat oil in pan. Roll drumsticks in wheatgerm or breadcrumbs, dip in beaten egg, then roll in wheatgerm or breadcrumbs again. Put chicken in pan, cover with lid and simmer for about 20 mins turning occasionally till brown all over.
Parsley sauce (see page 64).
20 - 25 minutes.

CURRIED LAMB AND RICE

1	Lamb cutlet (fat removed)
1	Small onion (peeled & chopped)
¼ pint	Water [62 ml]
1 tblsp	Vegetable oil
½ teasp	Onion seeds (obtainable from Chinese or Indian shops)
1 level tblsp	Sultanas
1 level dessert spoon	Curry powder
1 teasp	Worcestershire sauce
Pinch of	Ginger
	Salt & pepper to taste

1 heaped tablsp Long grain rice

Method

1. Lightly fry onion in oil until soft, add rest of ingredients, except chop and rice, and simmer gently for 15 mins.
2. Grill or fry chop slowly on medium heat, 7 mins each side.
3. Meanwhile make sauce and boil rice. Cover rice with water and season with salt. Bring to boil, reduce heat and simmer till soft, about 10 mins. Drain off water and serve with chop and the curry sauce.

20 - 25 minutes

FISH PANCAKE WITH TANGY SAUCE

4 oz	Cod or other white fish	[100 g]
1 heaped teasp	Plain flour	
1 knob	Margarine	
2 oz	Water (after cooking fish)	[50 ml]
2 oz	Milk	[50 ml]
½ teasp	Mustard	
½ teasp	Worcestershire sauce	
1 tblsp	Cream or yoghurt	
	Salt to taste	

Method

Cover fish in salted water and lightly steam for 5 mins. Drain off water and reserve for sauce. Flake fish and remove any bones. Cool. Melt margarine in saucepan and gradually stir in flour, then add the water and milk. Continue to stir to prevent lumps. Add rest of ingredients, except cream or yoghurt and fish, and simmer gently for 5 mins. Stir in the fish flakes and simmer for a further 5 mins. Gradually add the cream or yoghurt. If using yoghurt, do not boil or simmer as it will separate.
20 minutes.

Pancake

1 heaped tblsp	Plain flour	
Good pinch of	Salt	
1	Egg (beaten)	
2 oz	Water	[50 ml]
2 oz	Milk	[50 ml]

Method

Beat egg well, then add flour, salt, water and milk. Continue to beat the batter till nice and frothy. Leave to stand while the fish and sauce are being prepared. Rebeat the batter and pour about 1 tablespoonful of vegetable oil into frying pan, heat to smokey hot, then pour 2 tablespoonfuls of batter into pan. Brown on both sides. Spoon fish and sauce into pancake and fold over. Any batter left over will make another pancake for dessert with sugar and lemon or just syrup.
About 20 minutes.

FRYING PAN SOUFFLE

2	Eggs (separated)
2 slices	Lean bacon (minced & cooked)
2 tblsp	Mixed vegetables (for example, tomato, mushroom, onion, etc.)
	Salt & pepper to taste
Pinch of	Herbs

Method

Oil a small frying pan - or if you possess an omelet pan, all the better. Beat egg yoke up separately, add the herbs, then whisk up the egg whites separately. Now gently blend in the egg white with the yoke. Pour this into the pan and sprinkle vegetables over top. Lightly brown on one side till the top looks slightly spongy. Sprinkle bacon over vegetables, take the pan off the heat and put under the grill for a few minutes just to warm the vegetables thoroughly. Remove soufflé from pan and fold over in half on plate. Serve with one of the sauces (pages 57-67).

FISH PATTIES WITH CHEESE SAUCE

1 tblsp	Sunflower or corn oil
8 oz	Haddock fillets (cut into strips) [225 g]
1 clove	Garlic (optional)
	Salt & pepper
	Parsley and tomato for garnish
½ pint	Mashed potato [275 ml]
1	Egg
	Wheatgerm or breadcrumbs

Method

Cover fish with water, add salt and pepper and bring to boil, reduce heat and simmer for 5 mins. Drain off water. Blend fish and mashed potato till creamy. Beat egg. Roll fish and potato mixture into round shapes about 2½" wide. Dip in egg and roll in wheatgerm or breadcrumbs. Fry gently in shallow oil till nicely brown. Top with cheese sauce (see page 59), parsley, and tomato slices.
15 - 20 minutes

KEBABS

Kebabs can be made up with almost any kind of meat, diced into 1 inch squares or sausages, also cut into inch squares. You can also use bacon sliced rolled and fruit and vegetables, cut into chunks. Choose the amount of meat you want and thread the ingredients you have chosen onto two skewers. Whatever meat you choose, put this in the centre of the skewer, leaving the vegetables on the outer ends of the skewer.
Here is an example kebab -

2	Sausages (cut into chunks)
2 pieces	Bacon (rolled)
2	Mushrooms
2	Tomatoes
3 or 4 chunks	Cucumber
3 or 4 chunks	Red pepper

Alternatively use chunks of beef or lamp in place of sausage. Sprinkle the kebabs with salt and pepper, oil or butter and Worcestershire sauce. Cook under grill for about 20 mins. turning once or twice.

LAMB - CONTINENTAL STYLE

2 tblsp	Vegetable oil
½ lb	Lamb (boned and chopped into small pieces) [225 g]
1	Carrot (scraped & sliced into thin rings)
½ pint	Water
1	Small potato (chopped into chunks)
	Salt & pepper to taste
1 sachet	Bouquet garni
1	Stock cube
2	Criossants (obtainable from bakers and/or supermarkets)

Method

Heat oil in pan and brown lamb to seal in juices. Add rest of ingredients, except croissants, cover with lid, bring to boil, reduce heat and simmer gently for 1½ hours on a very low heat. Remove bouquet garni. Heat oven, put croissants on a baking sheet or pie dish and warm through for a few minutes. Serve on top of lamb, with vegetables in season.

*****

This dish is very nice served with dumplings instead of criossants for a change.
After lamb has cooked for 1¼ hours, make suet dumplings as follows -

1 tblsp	Shredded suet
2 heaped tblsp	Self raising flour
	Salt & pepper to taste
	A little water.

Method

Mix flour with suet and condiments. Add enough water to make a stiff dough. Roll into balls and arrange dumplings round stew. Replace lid and cook for further 15 minutes.
About 2 hours.

LIVER & BACON BURGERS WITH SAVOURY SAUCE

	Sunflower oil	
4 oz	Calves' or pigs' liver	[100 g]
1 slice	Bacon	
1	Small onion (chopped)	
1	Egg (beaten)	
2 tblsp	Red wine	
1 tblsp	Tomato ketchup	
1 level tblsp	Margarine	
1 heaped teasp	Plain flour	
¼ pint	Water	[62 ml]
1	Bay leaf	
Pinch of	Cayenne pepper	
2 heaped tblsp	Breadcrumbs or wheatgerm	

Method

Fry liver and bacon in oil till half done. Cool. Chop and blend or mince finely, till it is like a paste. Lightly fry onion. Beat egg and stir into liver, bacon and onion, leaving a little egg to dip the burgers into. Pat into rounds, dip into egg and roll in crumbs or wheatgerm. Lightly fry till brown and serve with savoury sauce (see page 65)
Garnish with parsley or watercress. Serve with boiled rice or pasta.
15 - 20 minutes.

MEAT PUDDING

½ lb	Chopped stewing steak	[225 g]
1 slice	Bacon (chopped and fat removed)	
1	Stock cube	
½ pint	Water	
	Salt & pepper	
Pinch of	Cayenne pepper	
	Flour	
	Vegetable oil	

Method

Oil small pudding basin or foil bowl. Roll chopped steak and bacon in flour and brown in oil for a few minutes in frying pan. Put in oiled basin, add enough stock to cover, then season with salt, pepper and Cayenne pepper. Any stock left over, use as gravy.

Pastry

4 oz	Self raising flour	[100 g]
2 oz	Shredded suet	[50 g]
	Salt & pepper	

Mix ingredients with enough cold water to make a stiff dough. Roll out or shape with fingers to size of top of basin. Cover with foil loosely to allow pastry to rise. Put basin in boiling water to about half-way up, and cover pan with lid. Reduce heat to gentle boil and keep topping up the pan with boiling water to keep the same level. Boil for 1½ hours. Serve with vegetables in season.

1½ hours

OMELET

1 or 2	Eggs
	Salt & pepper to taste
Pinch of	Cayenne pepper, thyme and onion salt
1 tblsp	Cheese (grated) or Chopped ham

Method

Whisk egg well, the add herbs and salt and pepper. Oil a frying pan - or an omelet pan if you have one. When oil is smokey hot, pour in the eggs. Keep heat fairly low. Run a spatula round pan to release omelet from side of pan. When omelet is slightly brown on one side, turn, sprinkle grated cheese, chopped ham, or leave it plain. Fold in half and serve. You can, of course, choose a sauce (pages 57-67) for extra luxury.

PORK - CHINESE STYLE

1	Pork shoulder steaklet (cut into $\frac{1}{4}$" slices)	
1 clove	Garlic (crushed)	
$\frac{1}{2}$ cup	Celery (chopped)	[100 g, 4 oz]
1	Small onion (chopped)	
2 tblsp	Vegetable oil	
1 heaped tblsp	Mushrooms (chopped)	
1 tblsp	Red pepper (deseeded & chopped)	
1 tblsp	Cucumber (chopped)	
1 level teaps	Cornflour	
1 teasp	Soy sauce	
1 cup	Chicken stock	[225 ml,8 oz]
1 cup	Bean shoots (obtained from Chinese shops and greengrocers)	[50g, 2 oz]
2 oz	Noodles or macaroni	[50 g]

Method

Put pork pieces in heated oil, brown lightly for about 10 mins on low heat. Add rest of ingredients, except bean shoots, stock and cornflour. Cover with lid and simmer for about 15 mins. Stir cornflour into stock and pour into pan with the bean shoots. Stir till thickened. Meanwhile, cook noodles or macaroni for about 5 mins in salted water. Drain noodles or macaroni and serve immediately with pork.

25 - 30 minutes.

PORK OR CHICKEN ESCALOPES WITH ORANGE SAUCE

½ lb	Pork fillet **or**	[225 g]
1	Chicken leg	
2/3 tablsp	Vegetable oil	
	Parsley or watercress for garnish	

Method

Melt oil in frying pan until smokey hot, then add the pork fillets, cover with lid and simmer gently till nicely brown. If using chicken, skin and break or cut into two sections and fry in the same way. Both need cooking for about 25 mins., turning occasionally to brown all over. Orange sauce (see page 63). Pour sauce over pork or chicken. Garnish with parsley or watercress.
25 - 30 minutes.

PORK STRIPS WITH BARBECUE SAUCE AND BOILED RICE

2	Pork strips (outer fat & rind removed)
1 tblsp	Vegetable oil.

Method

Heat the oil in frying pan and gently simmer pork strips. Cover with lid and simmer on low heat for 15 mins, turning once. Meanwhile prepare sauce (see page 58). Boil rice for 10 mins, drain and serve pork strips on rice, sauce poured over top and garnished with parsley.
15 - 20 minutes.

SAUSAGE PANCAKE AND MARROW SUPPER

1 slice	Bacon
3	Chipolattas (cut into pieces)
1	Small onion
	Salt & pepper
1	Egg
2 tblsp	Vegetable oil
¼	Small marrow (peeled, centre seeds and pulp removed)
	Watercress or parsley for garnish

Method

Heat vegetable oil in pan and lightly fry onion. Add sausages and bacon. Stir until done - about 5 mins on low heat. Whisk egg until frothy and add salt and pepper. Pour over sausage mixture and lightly brown. Turn and brown on other side.
Heat half oil in pin. Add chopped marrow and salt and pepper. Cover with lid and simmer for 15 mins. over low heat, stirring occasionally. Remove and serve with sausage pancake. Garnish with watercress or parsley.
15 - 20 minutes.

SAVOURY CROISSANT

1 or 2 Croissants
1 small tin Pimentoes [about 175-200 ml, 6-7 oz
2 oz Boiled bacon or ham (chopped) [50 g]
1 level teasp Sugar
2 heaped tblsp Diced pineapple
2 tblsp Pineapple juice
Salt & pepper to taste
Little cornflour to thicken

Method

Put all ingredients, except cornflour and croissants, into saucepan. Bring to boil, reduce heat and simmer for 10 mins, over a low heat. Lastly stir about 1 teaspoonful of cornflour into a little pineapple juice to a thick paste and blend into mixture. Mix well to prevent lumps forming until mixture is clear - about 3 mins. Heat croissant in oven for a few minutes, then slice in half and fill with savoury mixture.
About 10 minutes.

SAVOURY POTATO WAFFLES WITH PROVINCIAL SAUCE

1 tblsp	Vegetable oil, plus bacon rind & fat
	A little plain flour
2	Potato waffles **or**
2	Potato cakes (either bought from supermarkets or freezer centres)
1 level tblsp	Margarine or butter
1 teasp	Cream or yoghurt
1 teasp	Worcestershire sauce
1 level teasp	Cornflour
¼ pint	Milk [62 ml]
1 slice	Bacon (rind & fat removed)
¼ lb	Ham or boiled bacon (minced)[100g]
Pinch of	Mixed herbs
1 tblsp	White wine (optional)
1 clove	Garlic (optional)
	Parsley for garnish

Method

If making potato cakes, boil 2 medium potatoes in salted water for 10 mins, then mash with a little margarine and milk.Shape into squares and dust with flour. Fry in oil and bacon rind and fat. **Or** fry or grill potato waffles as directed on packet.

Sauce: Melt margarine in saucepan. Add cornflour gradually. Stir in a little milk at a time, then add wine. Blend in rest of the ingredients, except cream or yoghurt, stirring constantly to avoid lumping, over low heat for 10 mins. Lastly add cream or yoghurt.

Serve on waffles or potato cakes. Garnish with parsley.

20 - 25 minutes.

SAVOURY SAUTED MARROW WITH CHIPOLATAS

½	Small marrow (peeled, pulp & seeds removed)
1 clove	Garlic (optional)
2 tblsp	Tomato puree or ketchup
2 tblsp	Water
3	Chipolatas (sliced into ½" chunks)
1	Small onion (chopped)
1 tblsp	Margarine or cooking oil

Method

Slice marrow into half-inch chunks. Put all ingredients in saucepan and simmer for about 15 mins., or until marrow is soft. Serve with boiled rice (see page 34).
15 - 20 minutes.

SAVOURY WINTER PUDDING

2 oz	Minced beef	
1	Small onion (chopped)	
1 clove	Garlic (optional)	
2 oz	Cabbage or sprouts (chopped)	[50 g]
2 oz	Carrot (minced)	[50 g]
2 oz	Potato (mashed)	[50 g]
1	Potato (finely sliced)	
	Salt & pepper	
1	Stock cube, dissolved in 4 oz [100g] vegetable or tomato juice.	
	A little vegetable oil	

Method

Oil a fire-proof dish. Put mince on bottom of dish, then add all other ingredients in order, to make layers. Finally spread with sliced potato. Cover with lid or foil and bake in oven for about 30 mins at 190, 370F, Gas Mark 5, just above centre oven.
30 - 35 minutes.

SHRIMP OR PRAWN VOL AU VENT

2	Large frozen vol au vent cases	
1 level dessert spoon	Plain flour	
1 level dessert spoon	Margarine	
¼ pint	Milk	[60 ml]
About 6	Prawns or large shrimps (fresh or frozen)	
1 tblsp	Cream	
3 teasp	Prawn cocktail or seafood sauce	
3 teasp	Tomato ketchup	
1 clove	Garlic (optional)	
Good pinch	Cayenne pepper	
	Salt & pepper to taste	
	Watercress or parsley for garnish	

Method

Bake vol au vent cases as directed on packet. About 18 min 200, 435F, Gas Mark 7

Sauce: Melt margarine in saucepan, stir in flour and add milk, stirring constantly to prevent lumping. Add rest of ingredients, bring to boil, reduce heat and simmer for 10 mins. Spoon into vol au vent cases and garnish with watercress or parsley.

NOTE: Make sure prawns are properly defrosted before using.

20 -25 minutes.

SPAGHETTI BOLOGNESE

1 slice	Bacon (rind & fat removed.Chopped)	
1 tblsp	Vegetable oil	
6 oz	Mince (or Soya protein)	[175 g]
2 oz	Mushrooms (chopped)	[50 g]
½ level teasp	Dry mustard	
Good pinch	Oregano	
4 oz	Tomato juice	[100-125 g]
2 tblsp	Tomato ketchup	
2 tblsp	Red wine (optional)	
1	Bay leaf	
1 level teasp	Sugar	
	Salt & pepper	
1 clove	Garlic (chopped) (optional)	
4 oz	Spaghetti	[100-125 g]

Method

Heat oil and brown meat lightly. Add rest of ingredients and bring to boil. Reduce heat and simmer gently for 15 mins, over low heat.
Meanwhile, prepare spaghetti as direction on packet. When cooked, drain off water. Put Bolognese on top of spaghetti and sprinkle with Parmesan cheese (already grated in carton) or grated Cheddar cheese.
About 20 minutes.

TURKEY BREASTS OR STEAK OR CHICKEN FILLETS

Any of these can be bought from supermarkets. Fry 3 - 4 minutes on each side in oil - or as directed on packet - and serve with Cranberry herb sauce (see page 60). Serve with green peas. Total time about 10 mins.

Sauces

Experiment with the sauces and try them with different cuts of meat and fish, as well as vegetables. For instance, the curry sauce and barbecue sauce will go with both fish and meat – so chop and change and be adventurous.

BARBECUE SAUCE

1	Small onion (chopped)
1 tablsp	Vegetable oil
$\frac{1}{4}$	Red pepper (deseeded & chopped)
1 clove	Garlic (crushed) [optional]
1 teasp	Worcestershire sauce
Few drops	Tabasco
Pinch of	Cayenne pepper
$\frac{1}{2}$ teasp	Lemon juice
8 oz tin	Tomatoes (pips removed) [225 ml]
2oz	Mushrooms (chopped) [50 g]
	Parsley for garnish

Method

Heat oil in pan and gently brown onion, add the rest of the ingredients, cover with lid, bring to the boil, reduce heat and simmer for 10 min. Cool, then either sieve or put into a blender for a few minutes. Reheat sauce and serve with pork strips, chops, sausages or chicken.
10 - 15 minutes.

CHEESE SAUCE

1 level tblsp	Plain flour	
1 level tblsp	Margarine	
3 heaped tblsp	Grated strong cheese	
½ teasp	Dry mustard	
3 oz	Water	[75 ml]
3 oz	Milk	[76 ml]
	Salt to taste	

Method

Melt margarine in saucepan, stir in flour and gradually add rest of ingredients, except cheese, stirring constantly for 3 to 5 mins till it resembles a thick sauce. Lastly, add the cheese and stir till the cheese melts. Do not boil once the cheese has been added, as this tends to make the cheese rubbery. Serve with fish, patties or cauliflower.
7 - 10 minutes.

CRANBERRY HERB SAUCE

1 knob	Butter or margarine	
1 teasp	Plain flour	
¼ pint	Milk	[62 ml]
	Salt & pepper	
¼ teasp	Mustard	
1 teasp	Lemon juice	
Pinch of	Cayenne pepper	
1 level tblsp	Cranberry jelly	
1 tblsp	Red wine	
1 clove	Garlic (crushed)	

Method

Melt margarine in saucepan and stir in flour gradually, then add milk and stir till smooth. Add rest of ingredients. Bring to boil, reduce heat and simmer for 5 mins or until a good, smooth sauce. Serve with turkey breasts or chicken fillets. 7 - 10 minutes.

CURRY SAUCE

Good knob of Butter or margarine		
1 heaped tblsp Plain flour		
½ pint	Milk	[62 ml]
1 dessert spoon Curry powder		
1 teasp	Lemon juice	
1	Small onion (chopped)	
1 tblsp	White wine	
1	Hardboiled egg (mashed)	
Pinch of	Ginger	
	Salt to taste	

Method

Melt margarine in pan, stir in flour and milk, mix well till smooth. Add rest of ingredients. Bring to boil, reduce heat and simmer for 5 mins stirring constantly to prevent burning.
7 - 10 minutes

HOT SAVOURY SAUCE

Knob of Margarine
1 level dessert spoon Plain or Rice flour
4 oz Vegetable or tomato juice [100 ml]
½ teasp Dry mustard
1 tblsp Tomato ketchup
1 teasp Worcestershire sauce
Good pinch of Cayenne pepper
1 clove Garlic (crushed)
1 Small onion (finely chopped)
Salt & pepper to taste
1 tblsp Single cream

Method

Melt margarine, blend in flour and gradually add all other ingredients, except cream. Stir constantly for 3 - 5 mins till smooth and clear. Blend cream in last and serve with meat patties, turkey or chicken steaks or any kind of meat, except lamb.
7 - 10 minutes.

ORANGE SAUCE

1 heaped teasp Margarine
1 heaped teasp Plain flour
Salt to taste
Juice of 1 medium orange, plus enough added water to make up to 4 oz [150 ml], plus grated rind of orange
1 tblsp Brandy or sherry
1 clove Garlic (crushed) [optional]
1 slice Bacon (minced or chopped finely)
Pinch of Coriander
1 teasp Sugar

Method

Melt margarine in saucepan, lightly fry bacon, gradually stir in flour, then liquid ingredients. Continue to stir until clear and creamy, then add rest of ingredients. Bring to boil, reduce heat and simmer for 3 to 5 mins, stirring constantly until smooth. Serve with pork or chicken escalopes or turkey burgers.
7 - 10 minutes.

PARSLEY SAUCE

Either a packet of parsley sauce mix, with added parsley or -
1 heaped teasp Plain flour
1 heaped teasp Margarine
1 heaped teasp Parsley (fresh chopped)
Salt & pepper to taste
5 oz Milk [150 ml]

Method

Melt margarine in saucepan, then gradually add the flour, stirring constantly. Then add the rest of the ingredients and stir till the sauce is nice and creamy, about 3 to 5 mins. Serve with chicken or fish.
7 minutes.

SPICED APPLE AND CIDER SAUCE

1 Large Bramley or other cooking apple (peeled, cored & chopped)
1 level tblsp Sugar
¼ pint Cider [62 ml, 2½ oz]
1 heaped teasp Cornflour, or Rice flour
2 Cloves

Method

Place apple, cider and cloves in saucepan. Cover with lid and simmer till apple is soft. Add sugar and cook till sugar has dissolved. Then mix cornflour with a little cider to a thick paste. Mix in a stir till mixture thickens (about 5 mins). Serve with pork, sausages or chicken.
7 - 10 minutes.

SAVOURY SAUCE

1 level tblsp	Margarine	
2 tblsp	Red wine	
1 tblsp	Tomato ketchup	
1 heaped tblsp	Plain flour	
1	Bay leaf	
Pinch of	Cayenne pepper	
	Salt & pepper to taste	
$\frac{1}{4}$ pint	Water	[62 ml]

Method

Melt margarine in saucepan, add the flour and stir. Then, still stirring, gradually add the liquid and the rest of the ingredients. Simmer gently for 3 to 5 mins, or until the sauce is smooth and clear. Remove bay leaf. Serve with liver and bacon burgers or beefburgers.
7 - 10 minutes.

TANGY SAUCE FOR FISH PANCAKE

1 knob of	Margarine	
1 heaped tblsp	Plain flour	
½ teasp	Dry mustard	
½ teasp	Worcestershire sauce	
	Salt to taste	
2 oz	Fish water	[50 ml]
2 oz	Milk	[50 ml]
1 tblsp	Cream or yoghurt	

Method

Melt margarine in saucepan, then gradually stir in flour. Then add liquid and continue to stir and blend in rest of ingredients, except cream or yoghurt. Stir constantly till sauce is smooth and creamy (about 3 to 5 mins). Lastly blend in cream or yoghurt. Serve with fish pancake or other white fish.
7 - 10 minutes.

WHITE WINE SAUCE

White wine sauce may be made with the recipe for Chicken and ham (page) or it can be made separately with the same ingredients, but substituting water for stock, for other dishes. This recipe is for the separate sauce -

2 tblsp White wine
1 level tblsp Plain flour
6 tblsp Water
Salt & pepper to taste
2 tblsp Cream
Pinch of Tarragon

Method

Mix flour with a little of the water into a paste, then gradually add rest of ingredients, except cream. Bring to boil, then reduce heat and simmer for 3 to 5 mins, or until sauce is smooth and creamy. Lastly, add the cream. Serve with chicken, fish or omlette.

7 - 10 minutes.

Vegetables

Most vegetables freeze well and, of course, if you can freeze them yourself, they are much cheaper. This is very good for emergencies and those occasions when you don't want to spend the time preparing vegetables.
Having said that, it is much better to have fresh vegetables quickly cooked in the way I suggest, this being tasty as well as nourishing.
Some of the goodness is lost with freezing, but there is a lot to be said for both methods.

BRUSSELS SPROUTS

½ lb	Brussels sprouts	[225 g]
1 tblsp	Vegetable oil	
1 tblsp	Water	
	Salt & pepper to taste	
Pinch of	Sage for garnishing	

Method

Remove damaged outer leaves and wash sprouts thoroughly. Slice into thin layers. Heat oil in pan till boiling, season with salt and pepper. Carefully add sprouts, cover with lid. Stir occasionally for 5 mins. over medium heat, or until all the water has evaporated.Garnish with sage.
5 - 10 minutes.

BRUSSELS SPROUTS AND CARROTS

4 to 6	Sprouts
1	Fairly large carrot (Scraped & sliced into rings)
1 tblsp	Margarine
	A little cooking oil
	Salt to taste
	Mustard seeds to garnish

Method

Remove outer leaves of sprouts, wash and slice thinly. Heat cooking oil in frying pan, then add the margarine, but do not burn. Stir in the carrot and simmer over low heat for 5 mins. Add the sprouts and simmer for a further 5 mins. Add salt to taste, mix and serve with a knob of butter. Garnish with mustard seeds.
10 - 12 minutes.

BUTTER BEANS (dried)

1 heaped tblsp Butter beans, soaked overnight in water. Drain off water, then put beans in saucepan, cover with fresh water, seaon with salt. Cover with lid and bring to boil. Reduce heat and gently simmer over low heat for 20 - 30 mins., or until soft. Serve with a knob of butter.
About 20 - 30 minutes.

CABBAGE

½	Small cabbage
1 tblsp	Vegetable oil
1 tblsp	Water
Pinch of	Celery salt
	Salt & pepper to taste

Method

Damaged and outer leaves and heart stalk removed. Wash thoroughly. Slice into small pieces. Heat oil and water in pan till boiling. Carefully add cabbage, cover with lid. Stir occasionally for 5 mins over medium heat or until water evaporates. Add salt and pepper and celery salt.
5 - 7 minutes.

CABBAGE AND ONIONS

1	Small onion (peeled & sliced)
½	Small cabbage (washed & finely sliced)
	Salt to taste
	A little Worcestershire sauce

Method

Cover the bottom of a frying pan or wok with a little oil and water, then gently simmer onion over low heat until soft. If pan gets dry add a little more water. Flavour with salt, then add the cabbage. Cover with lid and gently simmer for about 5 mins, stirring occasionally to prevent sticking to pan. Lastly add Worcestershire sauce to taste.
About 10 minutes.

CABBAGE
PARSNIP OR CARROT PUREE

1	Small parsnip **or**
1	Medium carrot
1 tblsp	Margarine
	Salt to taste
	Marjoram for garnish

Method

Scrape carrot or peel parsnip. Cut into chunks. Put in saucepan, cover with water, add salt, bring to boil, reduce heat, then simmer for about 10 mins over low heat. Drain off water, cool and either blend for a few minutes or mash and sieve.Serve with butter or margarine. Garnish with marjoram.
About 10 - 12 minutes.

CAULIFLOWER WITH CHEESE

½	Small cauliflower	
1 level tblsp	Margarine	
1 level tblsp	Plain flour or rice flour	
4 oz	Milk	[100 ml]
2 oz	Water	[50 ml]
2 oz	Grated cheese	[50 ml]
½ teasp	Dry mustard	
	Salt & pepper	

Method

Break cauiflower into small pieces and wash. Put pieces into wok or frying pan and add water, salt and pepper. Bring to boil, reduce heat and simmer for 5 mins. covered with lid. Drain off any excess water. Arrange in fire-proof dish.
Cheese sauce: Melt margarine in saucepan, stir in flour to a thick paste, the gradually add the mustard and the liquid. Bring to boil, reduce to low heat and stir constantly for 3 mins to prevent lumps forming, then blend in the cheese. Do not boil the sauce after the cheese has been added or it will become leathery.
Pour over cauliflower and brown under grill.
15 minutes.

MIXED VEGETABLES

1	Carrot (sliced)
1	Small onion (peeled & chopped)
3 or 4	Brussels sprouts (cleaned & sliced)
1	Potato (peeled & diced into cubes)
Good pinch of	Nutmeg
Knob of	Margarine
	Salt & pepper to taste

Method

Put carrot in a wok or frying pan with lid and cover with water. Add salt & pepper to taste, cover with lid and simmer for 5 mins over low heat. Add the rest of the ingredients, cover with lid and simmer for a further 5 mins. This should be slightly crunchy.
10 - 15 minutes.

SAUTE POTATOES OR SWEET POTATOES (sometimes known as YAMS)

1 large potato or sweet potato, peeled and cut into clunks about 2". Put potato in saucepan, cover with water and salt to taste. Bring to boil, then reduce heat and simmer for 5 mins. Pour off water. Heat ¼ pint of cooking oil in a saucepan until smokey hot, then carefully add the potato. Cover with lid or foil, reduce heat, simmer gently, turning till the potato is nicely brown, for 10 to 15 mins. Pour off excess oil. PARSNIPS may be cooked in the same way.
15 - 20 minutes.

SPINACH

1 lb	Spinach	[450 g]
¼ pint	Water	[150 ml]
1 tblsp	Vegetable oil	
	Salt & pepper to taste	

Method

Wash and pick over spinach, discarding brown or soiled leaves. Break up spinach with fingers into small pieces and wash three or four times, or until water is clean. Heat oil and water. When water is boiling, carefully press in spinach with wooden spoon. Cover with lid and simmer for 5 mins. Strain spinach in colander, squeeze excess water out with wooden spoon. Serve with a knob of butter.
5 - 10 minutes.

Desserts

AUNT ETHEL'S FRUIT POM POM

1 teaspoon Lemon juice
2 heaped tblsp. of finely chopped mixed fruit
2 teasp. Chopped nuts
½ carton Double cream (small size) [150 ml 5 oz]
1 Cocktail cherry
2 level tblsp Icing sugar
Chocolate flavoured strands.
(suggested fruit - apple, orange, grapes, peaches, apricots, banana, cherries: about 100-125g - 4 oz)

Method

Whisk cream until it stands in peaks. Add half of icing sugar. Mix rest of sugar with fruit and lemon juice. Gently fold fruit into cream and spoon into serving glass, sprinkle chocolate strands over top and add cherry and nuts.

7 minutes.

BAKED SEMOLINA OR RICE PUDDING

1 heaped tblsp.	Either semolina or rice	
1 level tblsp	Sugar	
½ pint	Milk	[275-233 ml]
	Mace, nutmeg or cinnamon	

Method

Oil a fireproof dish and sprinkle semolina or rice into botom of dish, then add sugar and milk. Stir to blend the sugar into milk. Sprinkle either grated mace, nutmeg or cinnamon over top with a few dots of butter. Cover top with foil. Bake at 170, 325F, Gas·Mark 3 for 20 min

BANANA SPLIT

1	Banana
2 tblsp	Whipped cream
Some	Chopped nuts of your own choice
2 or 3	Cocktail cherries
	Chocolate strands

Method

Slice banana in half lengthwise. Spread cream over centre of banana. Garnish with chopped nuts, cherries and chocolate strands.

LEMON AND GINGER CRUNCH

2 oz	Crushed sweet biscuits	[50 g]
1 oz	Margarine or butter	[25 g]
Pinch of	Powdered ginger	
1 carton	Lemon frozen mousse (from supermarkets)	
A little	Vegetable oil	
A little	Crystallised ginger (chopped finely)	
A little	Whipped cream	
	Walnut for garnishing	

Method

Oil bottom and half way up the sides of an empty margarine tub (or small dish with sides). Mix biscuits and ginger together until it resembles a dough and press round bottom and sides of carton or dish. Place in 'fridge or freezer till hard. Scoop out mousse and spread over biscuits, top with chopped crystallised ginger and a little cream, plus some walnuts.
Takes about 5 minutes after removing biscuit base from refrigerator or freezer.

MARSHMALLOW CHOCOLATE DESSERT

1 level tblsp Syrup or apricot jam
2 Marshmallows
1 Shortbread biscuit
½ level teasp Instant coffee
2 teasp Water
½ small carton Double cream whipped [60 ml]
½ Flake bar **or**
2 portions Chocolate, finely grated [150 ml]

Method

Crumble biscuits finely into a serving glass. Melt marshmallow, coffee and water over gentle heat until runny (don't boil). Pour over biscuit. Whip cream, spoon over biscuit and top with jam, flake bar crumbled or grated chocolate. Chill and serve.
5 minutes.

RASPBERRY CREAM WHIRL

1 teasp	Cherry brandy (optional)	
½ small carton	Double cream	[60 ml; 2½ oz]
1 small carton	Raspberry frozen mousse	
	Raspberries and almond flakes for garnish	

Method

Whip cream. Scoop out raspberry mousse and place half in dessert glass, plus a few raspberries and cherry brandy. Pour half cream over and add rest of mousse and cream. Decorate with chopped raspberries and almond flakes.
5 minutes.

SPICED CREAM CROISSANT WITH NUTS

1 or 2	Croissant (bought from baker or supermarket)
$\frac{1}{2}$ carton	Double cream (small) [60 ml, $2\frac{1}{2}$ oz]
Pinch of	Cinnamon
1 level teasp	Crystallised ginger (finely chopped)
1	Cocktail cherry
1 level teasp	Chopped nuts
	Apricot or pineapple jam or Lemon curd

Method

Slice croissant in half. Spread with jam or lemon curd. Whisk cream and add cinnamon and ginger. Spread half cream on inside of croissant and rest on top. Sprinkle with nuts and cherry sliced in half.
About 5 minutes.

TRICIA'S CHOCOLATE CREAM SURPRISE

1 Chocolate frozen mousse (from supermarket)
$\frac{1}{2}$ small carton Double cream [60 ml. 2$\frac{1}{2}$ oz]
2 teasp Brandy or Rum
1 teasp Chopped walnuts
1 teasp Chocolate flavour sugar strands

Method

Spoon half the chocolate mousse into a serving glass. Whip cream, add brandy or rum and spoon half over mousse, then add rest of mousse and top with rest of cream, chocolate strands and nuts. Chill and serve.
3 - 5 minutes.

Cakes

COFFEE PARTY GATEAU

7 oz	Self raising flour	[200 g]
6 oz	Caster suger	[175 g]
6 oz	Margarine	[175 g]
3	Eggs (beaten)	
1 level tblsp	Instant coffee, dissolved in 1 tblsp hot water.	

Method

Cream margarine and sugar, add coffee, a little flour and mix. Add beaten eggs and rest of flour and mix well. Pour into a lined a greased 5" cake tin. Bake in just above centre oven at 180, 350F, Gas Mark 4 for 50 minutes. Raise temperature to 200, 400F, Gas Mark 6 and bake a further 15 minutes. Cool on rack. Slice in half and fill with coffee butter icing. Ice top of cake with coffee butter icing and decorate with walnuts.
For PLAIN PARTY GATEAU susbstitute 1 tblsp of lemon or orange juice or a teasp. vanilla essence for the Instant coffee.
1 hour, 10 minutes.

SPICED COFFEE OR CHOCOLATE FAIRY CAKES

¼ teasp	Vanilla	
¼ teasp	Cinnamon	
5 oz	Self raising flour	[150 g]
4 oz	Caster sugar	[100-125 g]
4 oz	Margarine	[100-125 g]

1 level dessert spoon Instant coffee, dissolved in 1 tblsp hot water

For Chocolate cakes substitute 1 oz [25 g] chocolate for one ounce of flour.

Method

Cream margarine and sugar. Add a little flour. Then beat in the eggs, add the vanilla and cinnamon and rest of flour. Beat well. Grease bun tins and divide mixture equally into 9 tins. Bake at 190, 370F, Gas Mark 5 for 15-20 mins. near top of oven. Decorate with coffee icing. 30 minutes.

SPICED SULTANA SCONES

8 oz	Plain flour	[225 g]
2 oz	Margarine	[50 g]
2 oz	Sugar	[50 g]
1	Egg (beaten)	
Pinch of	Salt	
3 teasp	Baking powder	
¼ pint	Milk	[62 ml]
½ teasp	Cinnamon or mixed spice	
2 oz	Sultanas	[50 g]

<u>Method</u>

Melt margarine and cool. Add all ingredients. Roll out to ¾" - 1" thick. Cut into 3" rounds. Bake at 230, 450F, Gas Mark 8 for 15-20 mins, near top of oven. Serve with cream and strawberry jam or syrup.

CHEESE SAVOURY SCONES

Leave out sugar and spice and add good pinch mixed herbs and 2 oz [50 g] grated cheese and ½ teasp dry mustard.
30 minutes.

WHEAT GERM AND BRAN LOAF

2 oz	All Bran	[50 g]
2 oz	Wheat germ	[50 g]
2½ oz	Sugar	[62 g]
2 tblsp	Syrup	
10 oz	Mixed dried fruit	[275 g]
¼ pint	Milk	[60 ml]
1	Egg	
4 oz	Self raising flour	[100-125g]
½ teasp	Vanilla essence	

Method

Whisk egg and mix with sugar. Add rest of ingredients and mix well. Line and oil a 5" cake tin. Bake at 350, 180F, Gas Mark 4, for about 1 hour, just above centre oven.

This bread is better after a couple of days keeping.

Note: a further 2½ oz of sugar can be substituted for the 2 tblsp. of syrup.

1 hour, 10 minutes.

Icings

For this book I have included only the most basic icing recipes. They are all quick and easy to prepare.

BUTTER ICING

8 oz	Icing sugar	[225 g]
2 oz	Butter	[50 g]
4 tblsp	Milk (approx)	

Method

Cream all the ingredients together until smooth and creamy. This is the basic icing. A few drops of flavouring essence may be added.

ORANGE ICING

Substitute undiluted orange squash or fresh orange juice for milk.

COFFEE ICING

Three tablespoons of coffee essence and one of milk, in place of four of milk.

CHOCOLATE ICING

1 tablespoon of cocoa, blended with 4 tablespoons of warm water in place of milk.

LEMON ICING

4 tablespoons of lemon juice in place of milk.

INDEX

Also by PATRICIA CARTER

AN ALLERGY COOKBOOK

Over 100 recipes for people who cannot tolerate milk, cheese, eggs, sugar, wheat or corn flour, butter, chocolate, salt or baking powder in their diet. Sensible advice is offered on how to check if a person is allergic to a certain ingredient and then appetising alternatives are presented.

£4.95

IAN HENRY PUBLICATIONS, Ltd.
38 Parkstone Avenue, Hornchurch Essex RM11 3LW